Sunny Weather

Written by Jillian Powell

Wayland

The sun and us

Most people like sunny weather. The sun can make us feel happy.

These children are enjoying sunshine in the playground.

Research shows that people are four times more likely to smile on a sunny day than a dull day! Do you smile more often in the sun?

The sun helps keep us healthy. In sunny weather, we tend to get more fresh air and exercise. Outdoor sports and games are more fun in the sun. Sunlight gives us vitamin D, which makes our hair, nails and teeth grow. Do you think your hair and nails grow faster in sunny weather?

Shadows and rainbows

You can only see your shadow when the sun is shining. Shadows are longest when the sun is low in the sky, in the morning and evening. They get shorter as the sun climbs higher in the sky. What happens to your shadow when the sun is almost overhead, at midday?

We see rainbows when it's sunny and rainy at the same time, because raindrops separate the colours of the **spectrum** which make up sunlight. There's an old saying:
A sunshiny shower won't last half an hour.
Try timing one!

The sun is fun!

Lots of people choose sunny places for their holidays. When it's warm and sunny, they can spend time outdoors, playing sports or sunbathing. In sunny weather, people enjoy eating outside too, taking a picnic to the beach or sitting at a café table, watching the world go by. You can have fun when the sun is shining.

People enjoy wearing light, bright clothes in sunny weather. Natural fabrics like cottons are coolest because they are woven and breathe better than **synthetics**. Light colours, especially white, are cool because they reflect the heat of the sun. Loose shapes, like baggy shirts and shorts, help the air to cool us.

Protecting against the sun

When our skin is exposed to the sun's rays, it produces a brown pigment called melanin which helps to protect it against burning. This is what we call 'sun-tanning'. The stronger the sun, the more melanin is produced, and the darker the skin becomes.

Many people like sunbathing, but too much sun can be dangerous. The sun's **ultraviolet** rays can burn and age our skin. Strong sunlight can also damage our eyes and cause sunstroke, giving us sickness and headaches. Sun creams help filter the sun's rays. Sunglasses and umbrellas can also be used to protect us from the hot sun.

Animal and plantlife and the sun

Some animals really enjoy sunbathing. Cats and dogs like sleeping in the sun. Marine animals like seals and walruses bask on rocks.

Cold-blooded reptiles like tortoises and lizards need the warmth and light of the sun to raise their body temperatures and give them energy.

Plants need sunlight to grow and to live. Green leaves take energy from the sun to **photosynthesize**. They combine carbon dioxide in the air with water to make the sugars they need to grow leaves and fruit. In hot weather, plants need more water as they lose moisture through their leaves to stay cool.

Stay cool!

Most villages in India have a special tree where people can shelter from the strong sunshine. In hot countries, it's usual for people to take a **siesta** or rest in the shade, in the middle of the day when the sun is hottest.

People find different ways to stay cool in hot, sunny weather. The sun makes us thirsty because we lose fluids when we perspire. Drinking cold drinks and eating ice-cream replaces lost moisture and makes us feel cooler. Sun-hats keep the hot sun off our heads. What do you do to stay cool?

Summer sun

How much sun we get depends on where we live and what time of year it is. Most parts of the world have a summer and a winter. The days are longer in summer because the sun rises higher in the sky at midday. When it is winter in the northern **hemisphere**, it is summer in the southern hemisphere, so Australians celebrate Christmas in the summer sun.

Long periods of hot, sunny weather, can bring problems. The earth dries up and plants like these sunflowers wilt from lack of water. If no rain falls, there will be a shortage of water. The use of hosepipes may be banned and some homes may lose their tap supply for a while.

The sun through glass

When the sun's rays shine through glass or some plastics, their heat is trapped. This is why it becomes very hot inside cars on sunny days.

No!

Never leave a dog in a car in hot weather. With windows closed and the sun blazing in, the car becomes like an oven, and the dog may die.

Many farmers and market gardeners use greenhouses to grow flowers, fruit and vegetables. The crops are protected from the cold and the wind, and the greenhouse traps the warmth of the sun even in the winter months, when there would not be enough warmth outside for crops to grow.

Harvest and drought

Crops need sunshine to ripen. Corn is ready to harvest when it has turned golden in the summer sun. Sun-ripened fruit is sweet and ready to eat.

◀ All fruit and vegetables need sunshine. These American children are choosing a ripe pumpkin for Hallowe'en.

People, animals and plants need sunshine to grow and live but they also need water. Everything loses moisture in the sun. The hotter and sunnier it is, the more moisture is lost. If there are long periods without rain in hot, sunny countries, people, animals and crops suffer from **drought**. Without water, they will die, like these animals in the Kalahari Desert.

Desert sun

In countries where it is hot and sunny all year round, and there is little or no rain, the land is a **desert**. Desert peoples have learnt to live with the hot sun. They wear long, loose clothes which are often white to reflect the heat. They cover their heads to protect themselves from the hot sun.

Camels are perfectly adapted to life in the desert. They can survive many days in the hot sun without drinking because they store fat in their humps which gives them moisture and energy. Their long, double rows of eyelashes keep out the glare of the sun.

Animal and plant adaptation

Desert animals have adapted to the hot sun in different ways. **Nocturnal** animals like the fennec fox and the kangaroo rat only come out to exercise and feed at night, when it's cooler. Others stay **dormant** for the hottest months of the year. Some animals and insects burrow underground, in the sand or under rocks, to escape the heat of the day.

Some plants are specially adapted to live in hot, sunny countries. Cactus plants store rainwater in their thick, fleshy stems. The largest cactus can store several litres of water!

Date palms (above) have very long roots which reach deep underground to find water.

Cities in the sun

In hot, sunny countries like Greece, houses are designed to keep out the heat. Thick walls are painted white to reflect the sun. Shutters shade windows. Some houses have wind towers which funnel cooling winds down into the house. Others have air-conditioning machines which suck in hot air and send out cool air.

Cities are often warmer than the surrounding countryside, because buildings store the sun's heat and warmth comes from fuel burnt in buildings and cars. In hot weather, cities can feel uncomfortably hot and airless. People living in cities often try to escape to the countryside for the hottest months.

The sun and the modern world

In hot, sunny weather, cities like London, New York and Tokyo suffer from high levels of pollution. The fumes from car exhausts and industry react with sunlight and heat to create **smog**. People are more likely to suffer from chest and breathing problems.

◀ New York

The sun's heat provides the world with a renewable source of energy. The solar power station in this photograph traps the sun's rays on giant reflectors. The heat boils water which drives the **turbines** to make electricity. Modern houses can also be built with solar panels on the roof, to provide electricity for heating and lighting.

Glossary

Cold-blooded Having a body temperature which is controlled by the environment. Reptiles, amphibians and fish are cold-blooded creatures.

Desert A dry region on earth.

Dormant Resting, not active.

Drought A long period of dry weather when no rain falls.

Equator An imaginary line encircling the earth midway between the North and South Poles.

Hemisphere Half of the globe, divided into North and South.

Nocturnal Active at night.

Photosynthesis The process by which plants combine carbon dioxide from the air with water to make sugars needed for growth.

Research A collection of information about something.

Siesta A rest, usually taken in the early afternoon in hot countries.

Smog A form of pollution, combining smoke with fog.

Spectrum The colours which together make up white sunlight: red, orange, yellow, green, blue, indigo and violet.

Synthetics Fabrics made from artificial, rather than natural materials.

Turbines Rotary motors driven by water, gas or steam.

Ultraviolet Invisible rays of light beyond violet on the visible spectrum.

Books to read

Bramwell, Martyn **Weather** (Franklin Watts 1987)

Gribbin, John and Mary **Weather** (Macdonald 1985)

Mason, John **Summer Weather** (Wayland 1990)

McInnes, Celia **Projects for Summer** (Wayland 1989)

Potter, Tony **BBC Factfinders Weather** (BBC Books 1989)

Rosen, Mike **Summer Festivals** (Wayland 1990)

Notes for parents and teachers

This series looks at four aspects of the weather with an interesting and informative approach. The specially chosen photographs reflect the author's innovative style involving the children directly with the subject. The clear and straight-forward text allows children to use the books independently, as a means for reference and as a resource.

These books relate closely to the National Curriculum offering support to any child embarking on Key Stage Two. Yet those children exploring the weather at home, can enjoy the many exciting ideas that invite discussion and question.

Suggestions for extension activities

1 Keep a diary of the weather. Compare it with the weather forecast. Was it the same? Try and forecast the number of sunny days in the next week.

2 Collect sayings and rhymes about the sun. Find out where they came from or how they originated. Do any of them seem to be true?

3 Have you seen a sundial? Find out how one works and see if you can make your own using cardboard.

Picture acknowledgements

The publishers would like to thank the following for allowing their photographs to be reproduced in this book: Bruce Coleman Ltd 7 (below/B. Coleman, 9 (above right/Keith Gunnar), 21 (Dr Eckart Pott), 28 (below/Jeremy Grayson); Chris Fairclough 8, 9 (below), 10 (above), 15 (main), 16, 17, 19 (above); Jimmy Holmes 14; Oxford Scientific Films Ltd 12 (top/Colin Milkins, middle/Okapia, below/Zig Leszczynski, 19 (below/Breck Kent, Earth Scenes), 20 (above/Ralph A. Reinhold Earth Scenes, below/Barbara Harrison and Alan C. Lane), 24 (inset/Warwick Johnson), 25 (above/Miriam Austerman, Animals Animals, below M.P.L. Fogden); Eye Ubiquitous 9 (above left/David Fobister), 10 (below/Rhoda Nottridge), 23 (below); Julia Waterlow 26 (below); Wayland Picture Library 4 (below); Tim Woodcock 6; ZEFA *cover*, 4 (above), 5, 7 (above), 11, 13, 15 (inset), 18, 20 (main), 22, 23 (above), 24, 26 (above), 28 (main), 29.

Index